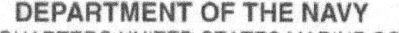
DEPARTMENT OF THE NAVY
HEADQUARTERS UNITED STATES MARINE CORPS
3000 MARINE CORPS PENTAGON
WASHINGTON, DC 20350-3000

I0440601

Classification Testing

DEPARTMENT OF THE NAVY
HEADQUARTERS UNITED STATES MARINE CORPS
3000 MARINE CORPS PENTAGON
WASHINGTON, DC 20350-3000

MCO 1230.5B
MPP
11 SEP 2009

MARINE CORPS ORDER 1230.5B

From: Commandant of the Marine Corps
To: Distribution List

Subj: CLASSIFICATION TESTING

Ref: (a) Marine Corps Manual (MARCORMAN)
       (b) MCO P1000.6G
       (c) MCO P1100.71A
       (d) MCO 1550.4D
       (e) MCO 7220.52E
       (f) Personnel Reporting Instructions Users Manual (PRIUM)
       (g) MCP 1130.52F
       (h) SECNAV M-5210.1
       (i) SECNAV M-5214.1
       (j) JAGINST 5800.7E

Encl: (1) Classification and Procurement Tests
       (2) Marine Corps Retest Policy
       (3) Marine Corps Test Facilities
       (4) ASVAB/AFCT Subtests and Marine Corps Composites
       (5) Current Language Testing Resources
       (6) Sample Inventory Format

Report Required: Inventory of Classification Test Materiel
                  (Report Control Symbol EXEMPT) par. 4b(2)(a)3

1. Situation. To provide information on the Marine Corps
Classification Testing Program and to publish standards and
procedures for the testing of Marines.

2. Cancellation. MCO 1230.5A.

3. Mission. To provide information on the classification and
personnel procurement test used in achieving the objectives set
forth in references (a) through (j). Reference (a) establishes
Marine Corps policy concerning the purpose, scope, and
application of personnel classification. Reference (b) provides
detailed instructions concerning the classification of military
personnel. Reference (c) contains instructions and procedures
for the enlistment or reenlistment of military personnel.
References (d) and (e) provide information on the Defense Foreign
Language Program and Foreign Language Proficiency Pay (FLPP).
Reference (f) provides instructions for reporting and correcting
of scores in the Manpower Management System. Reference (g) is a
joint directive which outlines testing policy for the Department
of Defense (DOD).

4. Execution

    a. <u>Commanders Intent and Concept of Operations</u>

        (1) <u>Commanders Intent</u>

            (a) The classification testing program is designed to estimate an individual's general mental ability and aptitude for a specific assignment or selection to a program.

            (b) Initial classification processing begins at the recruiting stations and at the MCRDs. Classification processing includes all interviewing and testing, as well as test and interview analysis.

                <u>1</u>. Individual interviews with each Marine are conducted to obtain information relative to the following areas:

                    <u>a</u>. Abilities, language skills, and aptitudes.

                    <u>b</u>. Military and civilian occupations.

                    <u>c</u>. Education/technical training.

                <u>2</u>. The objective of initial classification processing is to identify an individual's military potential and to make an initial assignment in consonance with manpower requirements.

            (c) Subsequent classification includes all classification actions taken after initial classification. The objective of subsequent classification is to meet the skill requirements associated with the manpower needs of the Marine Corps. This is done through the assignment of individuals to specific T/O billets as well as the reclassification, retraining, and reassignment of personnel consistent with their individual military potential. These objectives are achieved through the following actions:

                <u>1</u>. Interviewing Marines upon arrival at permanent duty stations to obtain the information indicated in paragraph 4a(1), and:

                <u>2</u>. To verify test score information on the Basic Training Record (BTR);

                <u>3</u>. To identify Marines requiring retesting. Unit commanders will ensure retests are administered to all active and reserve component Marines whose test scores are not resident in the Marine Corps Total Force System (MCTFS) and whose test scores cannot be retrieved from the Total Force Data Warehouse (TFDW) or Defense Manpower Data Center (DMDC).

(d) Classification tests are to be administered under the following circumstances:

<u>1</u>. To meet the prerequisites for assignment to formal schools, special duty assignments, and retraining in other Military Occupational Specialties (MOS).

<u>2</u>. To meet the basic requirements for reenlistment options.

<u>3</u>. To meet prerequisites for enlisted-to-officer programs.

<u>4</u>. To replace test scores not retrievable from the Marine Corps Total Force System (MCTFS) or the Official Military Personnel File (OMPF) held at HQMC.

(e) A Marine that has already attained the basic requirement for an assignment or program requiring a minimum classification test score will not be allowed to retest to increase their score.

(f) A consolidated list of classification and personnel procurement tests currently authorized for Marine Corps use is contained in enclosure (1). The procedures for requesting an in-service retest are contained in enclosure (2).

(2) <u>Concept of Operations</u>

(a) <u>Subsequent Classification Testing</u>

<u>1</u>. CMC (MPP-50) is responsible for all classification testing conducted subsequent to initial classification. All inquiries regarding subsequent classification testing that cannot be answered at the local testing facility or by the unit career retention specialist will be referred to CMC (MPP-50), DSN 278-9615/9616 or commercial (703) 784-9615/9616.

<u>2</u>. The following paragraphs provide brief descriptions of the standard classification tests authorized for Marine Corps personnel. These tests may be administered to any Marine (regular or reserve) who meets the eligibility requirements established in enclosure (2).

(b) <u>Standard Classification Tests</u>

<u>1</u>. <u>Armed Services Vocational Aptitude Battery (ASVAB)</u>. Since November 1976, the Marine Corps has used the ASVAB to classify and assign Marines. This test measures a Marine's aptitude and abilities necessary for successful performance on the job and during formal school training. Current editions of the ASVAB are used at Military Entrance

Processing Stations (MEPS) for initial classification testing of applicants within the Enlisted Testing Program (ETP). A brief explanation of the ASVAB, Marine Corps composite scores and subtests are explained in enclosure (4).

2. Armed Forces Classification Test (AFCT). On 1 October 1984, the AFCT replaced the ASVAB for in-service retesting of all DOD enlisted personnel. For the most part, the AFCT is the same test as the ASVAB and all scores are measured and interpreted in the same way.

3. General Classification Test (GCT). The GCT is administered in place of the ASVAB/AFCT for all commissioned and warrant officers and is administered at The Basic School. Scores are used to measure the mental aptitude of officers and play a significant role in the selection of one's MOS. After MOS selection, the GCT is generally used as a metric for measuring the intellectual health of the officer corps. In-service retests of the GCT are not authorized and this test should not be used as a metric for assignment or selection to any program once an officer graduates from The Basic School.

(c) Special Classification Tests

1. Defense Language Proficiency Test (DLPT). The DLPT is designed as the standard test for determining proficiency in a foreign language as required by reference (e). The DLPT is a web-based exam which contains two subtests: reading and listening. Scores are based on the Interagency Language Roundtable (ILR) scale and are used to determine FLPP as determined in reference (e) as well as to determine assignments and selection to programs requiring a language skill. A list of current language testing resources is contained in enclosure (5). CMC (IOP) is the sponsor for the Marine Corps Foreign Language Program and thus manages the FLPP Program.

2. The lower level DLPT is graded on a 0 to 3 level on the ILR scale. In instances where a language has a lower level and upper level version of the DLPT, one must first attain a score of 3 on the lower level test before taking the upper level test for that particular language.

3. The upper level test rates a Marine's proficiency from a 3 to 4 on the ILR scale. The upper level test needs to be completed within 90 days following the administration of the lower level exam. If the Marine does not retest within 90 days, then that Marine will not be allowed to take the upper level version of the test until successfully completing the lower level test which may be administered no earlier than 6 months following the completion of the last lower level test. However, if a Marine posts a score of 3+ or higher on an upper level DLPT, then that Marine may continue to retest at the upper level as

long as that Marine continues to attain a score of 3+ or higher on that test.

(d) <u>Oral Proficiency Interview (OPI)</u>. The Speaking skill is tested with the OPI, a task-based test that measures performance according to the ILR level descriptions. The OPI includes four phases: the warm-up, level checks, probes, and a wind-down. The warm-up establishes interaction and rapport between testers and the examinee. Level checks identify those language functions and content areas the examinee can handle. Probes are used by testers to raise the level of the examinee's language and determine a ceiling for his or her speaking ability. The wind-down returns the examinee to a comfortable level of conversation and gives the tester the opportunity to ensure the examinee is properly graded on the ILR scale. The speaking portion of the test will only be given upon request by CMC Intelligence Operations and Personnel (IOP). CMC (IOP) is the sponsor for the Marine Corps Language Program and thus manages the FLPP Program. The OPI rates a Marine's proficiency from a 0 to 5 on the ILR scale.

(e) <u>Defense Language Aptitude Battery (DLAB)</u>. The DLAB is designed to measure a Marine's potential to learn a foreign language and to aid in the selection of personnel for language school training. The DLAB may be taken by personnel applying for or being considered for assignment to language training. In accordance with reference (i), the DLAB is required for PMOSs 02XX/26XX.

(f) <u>Confirmation Tests</u>

<u>1</u>. In the event a Marine shows a significant gain on a classification test of 20 or more points on any composite score on the AFCT, 40 or more points on the AFQT, doubles the AFQT within a year timeframe, 20 or more points on the DLAB, or 2 points on the ILR scale for the DLPT, those test results will be subject to review by the Testing and Measurement Control Officer (TCO), CMC (MPP-50). If the TCO determines that there is significant reason to question the results of those scores, the TCO may notify the Marine via his/her chain of command that those results are being held in lieu of successful completion of a confirmation test.

<u>2</u>. The scoring of the confirmation test follows a simple formula. The Marine must obtain half the number of points associated with a significant gain to confirm the prior scores. In other words, if a Marine initially scored a 0 on the AFQT then scores a 100 on the retest, the Marine will only need to score a 50 on the confirmation test to retain the AFQT score of 100. If the Marine scores a 49, then the 0 will remain the score of record. These results will be passed by the TCO to the Marine via the chain of command with any recommendations for administrative action for the unit commander.

b. Subordinate Element Missions

(1) Marine Corps Test Facilities

(a) Test materiels are provided to test facilities by CMC (MPP-50). Commands not designated as a test facility (refer to enclosure (3)), and not covered under the cognizance of a test facility, must notify CMC (MPP-50) of the need to test a Marine.

(b) All test booklets, answer sheets, scoring keys, and other associated classification test materiel are controlled items. Commanders of the test facilities listed in enclosure (3) are responsible for the control and security of all testing materiel in their custody. They will issue written instructions to ensure the establishment of sound security and compromise prevention measures as follows:

1. An officer, SNCO, or civilian GS-7 (or higher) will be designated in writing as the Classification Test Materiel Custodian (CTMC). A certified true copy of the designation will be forwarded to the CMC (MPP-50) no later than 30 days after assignment.

2. A SNCO, NCO, civilian GS-5 (or higher) or a civilian contractor will be designated in writing as the Testing Administrator. A certified true copy of this designation will be forwarded to CMC (MPP-50) no later that 30 days after assignment.

3. Unit career retention specialists are not eligible to be appointed as CTMC's or Test NCO's.

4. All classification testing materiel will be stored in safes or vaults when not in use. Combinations for these safes/vaults will be changed on the following occasions:

a. When the safe/vault is originally placed in use for storage of classification test materiels.

b. When personnel (military or civilian) who have knowledge of the combination are no longer authorized or require access.

c. When the combination has been subject to possible compromise.

d. At least once semiannually.

(2) Classification testing materiel will be inventoried as follows:

(a) Semiannually, during June and December

1. The CTMC will ensure that all classification testing materiel is accounted for and, when practical, a page-check of each item will be made.

      2. The CTMC will evaluate testing materiel storage areas for proper security during each semiannual inventory. The evaluation results will be incorporated into that inventory. Evaluation results of the storage area should include the type of container(s) being utilized for storage, a description of the storage area, and accessibility during working and off-duty hours.

      3. The originals of the semiannual inventories conducted will be forwarded to CMC (MPP-50). These inventories are due to CMC (MPP-50) by the 15th of the following month. This reporting requirement is exempt from reports control according to reference (i), part IV, paragraph 7n.

      (b) Upon relief of a CTMC, a joint inventory of all testing materiel will be conducted by the current CTMC and the person relieving the CTMC. This turnover inventory and a certified true copy of the new CTMC's designation letter will be forwarded to CMC (MPP-50) within five (5) days of appointment.

      (3) Compromise/Possible Compromise, Loss, Accidental Destruction, or Misuse of Test Materiel. The compromise or possible compromise, loss, accidental destruction, or misuse of classification testing materiel will be reported immediately to the Testing Measurement and Control Officer at CMC (MPP-50) via priority message or an encrypted, digitally-signed e-mail. Test forms involved will immediately be suspended from use in that geographical area and a statement to that effect will be included in the message. The suspended test forms will not be placed back in use until authorized by CMC (MPP-50). An officer or SNCO, other than the custodian, will be appointed per reference (j), Manual of the Judge Advocate General, to inquire into the circumstances surrounding any compromise/possible compromise, loss, accidental destruction, or misuse of test materiel. Upon completion of the investigation, the commander will forward a completed copy of the investigation, via the chain of command, to CMC (MPP-50). If the investigation cannot be forwarded within 60 days, the CTMC will notify CMC (MPP-50) of the circumstances surrounding the delay.

      (4) When not in the possession of the person being tested, test materiel will only be handled by the CTMC or the testing administrator.

      (5) Marine Corps Classification Test Facilities have been established by CMC in locations throughout the world to ensure adequate testing/retesting of Marine Corps personnel. In order to maintain standardized testing procedures and ensure a high quality of testing, each test facility should:

      (a) Have adequate room allotted to ensure each examinee has a minimum working space of 36 by 15 inches.

      (b) Have flat, level writing surfaces (table tops). Chairs with writing arms are not considered adequate for testing purposes.

(c) Be well-ventilated and maintain a comfortable temperature year round.

(d) Be free of external distractions (i.e., heavy personnel traffic, machinery, etc.).

5. Administration and Logistics

a. Administration Instructions for Classification Tests within the Regular and Reserve Establishments

(1) Only those test facilities listed in enclosure (3) are authorized to hold classification testing materiel on a continuing basis. This authority cannot be delegated to subordinate commands or units.

(2) Personnel who are familiar with, or have had access to classification test materiels (i.e., CTMCs, Test Administrators, test facility personnel, recruiters, etc.) are not authorized to test/retest until a period of 2 calendar years has elapsed from the date of their reassignment from that position. Requests for waivers to this requirement must be submitted in writing to CMC (MPP-50) for consideration, and must contain all information required in enclosure (2).

(3) Marines will be retested per the instructions in enclosure (2) and will not be retested earlier than 6 months following the most recent retest. Exceptions to those requirements can only be authorized by CMC (MPP-50) and will not be entertained unless a minimum of 90 days have passed from the last retest date. Once an individual has started a language or classification test, it must be completed unless extenuating circumstances exist. In the event the person being tested does not desire to complete a test, the test will be forwarded to CMC (MPP-50) with an explanation. CMC (MPP-50) will determine if a justifiable reason exists for the test not being completed. If none exists, the test scores obtained from the incomplete test will become the official scores of record.

(4) Marine Corps personnel are authorized to retest at a Military Entrance Processing Station (MEPS) but are not authorized to retest at a Military Entrance Test (MET) site. Marines who desire to retest at any testing facility established by MEPCOM or other component of the Armed Forces must first obtain written authorization from their Commanding Officer (Bn/Sqdn level). This authorization will considered and if approved will be forwarded to the appropriate testing facility by CMC (MPP-50). Retesting at a Marine Corps test facility remains the preferred method for all classification testing since this ensures that all test results are received and processed in a timely manner.

(5) Classification test materiel is for "OFFICIAL USE ONLY". Accountable test materiel (test booklets, scoring keys, test tapes, and scored answer sheets) will be transmitted by Federal Express. If no Federal Express account exists, then the materiel must be sent via "CERTIFIED" (not registered) mail or hand-carried. Completed or partially completed answer sheets, which have not been scored, may be transmitted via certified mail to the CMC (MPP-50) for processing. If certified mail is used, a "Return Receipt" must be requested. Parcels containing classification testing materiel must be double-wrapped, tape-sealed, and accompanied by a signed letter of transmittal on command letterhead. The inner wrapper will be clearly marked in such a manner as to identify the contents as "For Official Use Only - Classification Test Materiel - To Be Opened by Authorized Personnel ONLY". The letter of transmittal will include a statement or enclosure which lists the test materiel transmitted. Test booklets will never be transmitted in the same package with scoring keys. The official mailing address for CMC (MPP-50) is:

Commandant of the Marine Corps
Manpower and Reserve Affairs (MP)
Attn: MPP-50 Testing
3280 Russell Road
Quantico, VA 22134-5103
OFFICIAL BUSINESS

    b. <u>Test Scoring and Reporting Procedures</u>

       (1) <u>Accession Testing</u>. Accession testing, which encompasses the Career Exploration Program, the Enlistment Testing Program, and the administration of special classification tests is administered by the MEPS in accordance with MEPCOM regulations. Test scores for all non-prior service and prior service personnel are entered into the MEPCOM data base for retention. Once accessed, those scores are loaded into the Marine Corps Recruit Information Support System (MCRISS) for transfer into MCTFS for input into the Marine's record. Test scores for prior service personnel, not required to attend Marine Corps recruit training, must be forwarded to CMC (MPP-50) for input into MCTFS.

       (2) <u>In-Service Retesting Scoring Procedures</u>. All in-service retests of Marine Corps personnel will be machine/hand-scored by CMC (MPP-50) to become part of their official record.

       (3) <u>Reporting Procedures</u>

          (a) Classification test answer sheets received by CMC (MPP-50) will be machine/hand-scored, entered into MCTFS, and retained on file for a period of six (6) months.

           <u>1</u>. Upon the administration of a subsequent classification test, and within a period of 30 days after receipt by the CMC (MPP-50), the parent unit may view the scores on the TEST screen of MCTFS.

2. In cases where test scores have not posted to MCTFS within 45 days of the test date, units should contact the CMC (MPP-50) for guidance and assistance. Under no circumstance should units or individuals contact CMC (MPP-50) for test score information prior to 30 days after testing or for information which could otherwise be determined through unit level MCTFS inquiries.

(b) Reporting of classification test scores via the unit diary is not authorized by field commands. Classification test scores can only be input into MCTFS by CMC (MPP-50).

(c) The Basic Training Record (BTR) and the TEST screen of MCTFS will contain the Marine's most recent test scores. Reporting units finding discrepancies in test scores will notify CMC (MPP-50) to request corrective action.

c. Supply of Classification Testing Materiel

(1) Each test facility will maintain enough classification testing materiel as needed to provide the geographical location with adequate testing support. The amount of test materiel requested by each classification test facility will be validated and approved by CMC (MPP-50).

(2) When a decrease in the amount of test materiel is desired, or when testing materiel becomes unserviceable, replacements will be requested from CMC (MPP-50). Upon receipt of new materiel and authority from CMC (MPP-50), the old test materiel will be destroyed locally by the CTMC. A destruction report, containing the following information, will be provided to CMC (MPP-50):

(a) Date of destruction.

(b) Means and location of destruction.

(c) Test materiel destroyed (to include serial numbers of each item).

(3) Test facilities will maintain at least a 90-day supply of classification test answer sheets. Classification test answer sheets identified as a "NAVMC" form must be requisitioned through local supply channels. Any other classification test answer sheet forms must be requested from CMC (MPP-50).

(4) Reproduction of any classification test materiel (to include completed answer sheets), whole or in part, is prohibited without written authorization from CMC (MPP-50).

d. Satellite Test Facilities

(1) In the past, satellite test facilities were established to allow classification testing in areas which would otherwise cause hardship to the personnel who require testing.

With the advent of web-based classification testing and agreements with other Services within the Department of Defense, the only authorized Marine Corps parent test facility to maintain satellite test facilities is the Marine Embassy Security Group.

(2) Satellite test facilities may only be established by CMC (MPP-50).

(3) The parent test facility is responsible for ensuring that all satellite test facilities properly secure, administer, and forward test materiels for processing.

(4) Satellite test facilities will submit their annual inventory to the parent test facility for preparation of a consolidated inventory. The annual inventory submitted by the parent test facility will indicate what materiel has been sub-custodied to each of its satellite test facilities.

e. <u>Violation of Testing Procedures</u>. Compliance with the provisions of this Order is mandatory for all Marine Corps Test Facilities to preclude loss and/or compromise of classification test materiel. Noncompliance with these provisions may result in the termination of status as a test facility or denial of requests for testing materiel.

f. <u>Records Disposition</u>. The following records disposition instructions are established:

(1) Records relating to the inventory of classification test materiel will be retained onboard and destroyed upon completion of the next inventory.

(2) Records relating to reporting/investigating of compromise/possible compromise, loss, accidental destruction, or misuse of classification test materiel will be retained onboard and destroyed 2 years after the end of the calendar year involved.

(3) Records relating to the assignment of a CTMC and Testing NCO will be retained onboard and destroyed 1 year after completion of assignment.

(4) Records relating to requests for retesting/waivers of tests or records relating to an increase/decrease in the amount of test materiel will be retained onboard and destroyed 1 year after the end of the calendar year involved.

(5) Records used as supporting documentation for unit diary reporting will be retained onboard and destroyed 6 months after the date the score is run on the unit diary per reference (h).

6. <u>Command and Signal</u>

a. <u>Command</u>. This Order is applicable to the Marine Corps Total Force.

b. <u>Signal</u>. This Order is effective the date signed.

Deputy Commandant for
Manpower and Reserve Affairs

DISTRIBUTION: PCN 10200810200

CLASSIFICATION AND PROCUREMENT TESTS

CLASSIFICATION TEST OR TEST BATTERY	TEST EMPLOYMENT	COGNIZANT CMC CODE	PERTINENT DIRECTIVE
Armed Service Vocational Aptitude Battery (ASVAB) Forms Screening	Enlistment/ Officer	MPP-50	MCO P1100.75C MCO P1100.73B
Armed Service Vocational Aptitude Battery (ASVAB) Form 18/19 (HS Test)	Enlistment Screening	MPP-50	MCO P1100.75C MCO 1130.52F
Armed Forces Classification Test (ASVAB 18F/19G)	Enlisted Classification	MPP-50	This Order
General Classification Test (GCT) Forms 3A/3B	Officer Classification	MPP-50	This Order
Defense Language Proficiency Test III/IV/ V (DLPT III/IV/V)	Officer/ Enlisted Classification	MPP-50/ IOP	This Order
Defense Language Aptitude Battery (DLAB)	Officer/ Enlisted Classification	MPP-50/ IOP	This Order
Scholastic Aptitude Test (SAT) and American College Test (ACT)	Officer Screening	MRO	MCO P1100.73B MCO 1560.15L

Enclosure (1)

MARINE CORPS RETEST POLICY

1. All Marine Corps Test Facilities are directed to follow the guidelines established in this enclosure prior to retesting a Marine.

2. **NO MARINE** will be allowed to retest without first obtaining written authorization from his/her command at the battalion/squadron level (see sample letter below). These requests may be signed "By direction" from the unit career retention specialist or any staff officer with "By direction" authority from the Commanding Officer.

3. All in-service retest requests will be submitted to the Marine Corps Test Facility with a printout copy of the Marine's current test scores in MCTFS. This sheet will be used to verify the need to retest for a particular assignment or program. If this sheet is not forwarded with the Marine's answer sheets and authorization letter, the Marine's retest scores will not be run on unit diary.

4. Marines will not be retested earlier than 6 months following the most recent retest. Exceptions to this requirement can only be authorized by CMC (MPP-50) and will not be entertained unless a minimum of 90 days have passed from the last retest date and a formal request has been sent by that Marine's command. Marines who participate in the Military Academic Skills Program (MASP) may retest after 90 days have passed from the date of the last retest; however, these Marines still need to request a retest waiver from CMC (MPP-50).

<u>Request for In-Service Retest of Classification Test (Sample)</u>

1230
Office Code
Date

From: Commanding Officer/Officer In Charge
To: Education Officer, Marine Corps Base Quantico

Subj: REQUEST FOR INSERVICE RETEST OF CLASSIFICATION TEST

Encl: MCTFS Print-out of Scores for Sgt I. M. Motivated

Ref: (a) MCO 1230.5B

1. In accordance with the reference, request an in-service
retest of the Armed Forces Classification Test/Defense Language
Proficiency Test. Sgt I. M. Motivated is applying for the
Warrant Officer Program and needs to attain an EL score of 110.
His current score is a 108 and he last tested on 28 January 2006.
Attached is a certified true copy of his TEST screen from MCTFS
verifying these scores.

2. Point of Contact for this request is Major I. M. InCharge,
Commanding Officer, Marine Unit, Overseas at (123) 456-7890, DSN
456- 7890.

I. M. INCHARGE
(or By direction)

MARINE CORPS TEST FACILITIES

East Coast Installations	West Coast and Hawaii Installations	OCONUS and I &I Duty Installations
Marine Corps Combat Development Command (MCCDC) Commanding General (Attn Education Office) 3088 Roan Street Quantico, VA 22134 COMM: 703-784-4010 DSN 278-4010	Marine Corps Logistics Base (MCLB) Barstow Commanding Officer (Attn: Lifelong Learning) PO Box 110600 Barstow, CA 92311-5047 COMM: 760-577-6118 DSN: 282-6118	Marine Corps Air Station (MCAS) Iwakuni Commanding Officer (Station Education Office) Marine Corps Air Station Iwakuni Japan PSC 561 Box 791 FPO AP 96310-0018 COMM: 011-81-6117-53-3855 DSN: 315-253-3855
Headquarters Battalion, Henderson Hall Commanding Officer (Attn: Education Officer) Headquarters Battalion Henderson Hall 1555 S. Southgate Road Arlington, VA 22214-5001 COMM: 703-614-9104 DSN: 224-9104	Marine Corps Base (MCB) Camp Pendleton Commanding General (Attn: Joint Education Center) Box 55020 Camp Pendleton, CA 92055-5020 COMM: 760-725-6660/6414 DSN: 365-6660/6414	Marine Corps Base (MCB) Camp Butler Commanding Officer Base Education Office Marine Corps Base Camp Butler Okinawa, Japan, Unit 35042 FPO AP 96373-5042 COMM: 011-81-6117-45-7160 DSN: 315-645-7160
Marine Corps Air Station (MCAS) Cherry Point Commanding General Training Support Department PSC Box 8019 Marine Corps Air Station Cherry Point, NC 28533-0019 COMM: 919-466-5195/3500 DSN: 582-5195/3500	Marine Corps Recruiting Depot (MCRD) San Diego Commanding General (Attn: Base Education Office) Marine Corps Recruiting Depot 4025 Tripoli Ave Bldg 111 San Diego, CA 92140-5001 COMM: 619-524-6865 DSN: 524-6865	MARFORRES, New Orleans, LA Commanding Officer Marine Reserve Forces 4400 Dauphine Street New Orleans, LA 70146-5400 COMM: 504-678-4396 DSN:678-4396

East Coast Installations	West Coast and Hawaii Installations	OCONUS and I &I Duty Installations
Marine Corps Recruit Depot (MCRD) Parris Island Commanding General (Attn: MCCS Education Center) PO Box 5100 Bldg 923 Marine Corps Recruit Depot Parris Island, SC 29905 COMM: 843-228-2132 DSN: 335-2132	Marine Corps Air Station (MCAS) Yuma Commanding Officer (Attn: MCCS Lifelong Learning) Marine Corps Air Station Box 99132 Yuma, AZ 85369-9119 COMM: 928-269-3248/3589 DSN: 269-3248/3589	COAST GUARD OR NAVY BASES If you're aboard a Coast Guard or Navy Installation, visit their local education center.
Marine Corps Logistics Base (MCLB), Albany Commanding General (Attn: MCCS Education Center) 814 Radford Bldg Suite 2033 Marine Corps Logistics Base Albany, GA 31704-0333 COMM: 912-639-5162 DSN: 567-5162	Marine Corps Base (MCB) Kaneohe Bay Commanding General (Attn: Education Officer, ESO) Box 63077 Marine Corps Base, Hawaii Kaneohe Bay, HI 96863-3077 COMM: 808-257-6730/1232/2158 DSN: 457-6730/1232/2158	

Enclosure (3)

ASVAB/AFCT SUBTESTS AND COMPOSITES

1. The ASVAB subtests are designed to measure aptitudes in five domains: Verbal, Math, Science, Technical, and Spatial. The table below describes the content of the ASVAB subtests. The subtests are presented in the order in which they are administered. The eight ASVAB subtests are:

    a. <u>General Science - GS</u>. A 25-item test measuring knowledge of life science, earth and space science, and physical science

    b. <u>Arithmetic Reasoning - AR</u>. A 30-item test measuring ability to solve basic arithmetic word problems

    c. <u>Word Knowledge - WK</u>. A 35-item test measuring ability to understand the meaning of words through synonyms

    d. <u>Paragraph Comprehension - PC</u>. A 15-item test measuring ability to obtain information from written materiel

    e. <u>Mathematics Knowledge - MK</u>. A 25-item test measuring knowledge of mathematical concepts and applications

    f. <u>Electronics Information - EI</u>. A 20-item test measuring knowledge of electrical current, circuits, devices, and electronic systems

    g. <u>Auto and Shop Information - AS</u>. A 25-item test measuring knowledge of automotive maintenance and repair, and wood and metal shop practices

    h. <u>Mechanical Comprehension - MC</u>. A 25-item test measuring knowledge of the principles of mechanical devices, structural support, and properties of materiels

    i. <u>Verbal - VE*</u>. The sum of the Word Knowledge and Paragraph Comprehension subtests.

2. There are five composite scores the Marine Corps uses to measure one's military potential. The AFQT is the only composite score used by the Marine Corps that is shared by all branches of the Armed Services. While all Services have a General Technical (GT) composite score, each service uses a different formula to compute these scores; therefore, be careful not to confuse the Marine Corps GT score with that derived by other services. When a Marine tests at another Service's testing facility, all scores posted on the testing memorandum are generally done under the guidelines of that service. The composite scores will change once graded by CMC (MPP-50). The five Marine Corps composite scores are:

AFQT = 2*VE + AR + MK

GT - General Technical   WK + PC + AR + MC

MM - Mechanical Maintenance   AR + EI + MC + AS

EL - Electronics Repair   AR + MK + EI + GS

CL - Clerical/Administration   WK + PC + MK

Current Language Testing Resources

This list is current as of 17 March 2009. This list will be updated as new tests are fielded.

Language	Digraph LIC	DLPT	DLIFLC	ACTFL	FSI In-Hse	FSI Outside
Afrikaans	AA					√
Albanian	AB	√	√		√	
Amharic	AC	√		√		√
Arabic-Eastern	QE				√	
Arabic-Egyptian	AE	√	√	√	√	
Arabic-Gulf (includes Arabic spoken in Iraq, Oman, Qatar, Bahrain, Kuwait, NE Saudi Arabia, and S. Iran)	DG	√	√	√		
Arabic-Jordanian (see Arabic-Levantine)	AK					
Arabic-Lebanese (see Arabic-Levantine)	AQ					
Arabic-Levantine (includes sub-dialects of Syrian, Jordanian, Lebanese, and Palestinian)	AP	√	√	√	√	
Arabic-Libyan	AL			√		
Arabic-Maghrebi* (see Arabic-Tunisian/Moroccan)	AM					
Arabic-Modern Standard	AD	√	√	√	√	
Arabic-Moroccan (sub-dialect of Maghrebi)	BS		√			
Arabic-Omani (See Arabic-Gulf)			√			
Arabic-Palestinian (see Arabic-Levantine)	Not assigned		√	√		
Arabic-Sudanese (inc. Saudi)	AV		√		√	
Arabic-Syrian (see Arabic-Levantine)						
Arabic-Tunisian (sub-dialect of Maghrebi)	BW		√			
Arabic-UAE (See Arabic-Gulf)			√			
Arabic-Western	QM				√	
Arabic-Yemeni	AU			√		
Armenian-Eastern Only	AR				√	
Armenian-Western/Eastern	AR		√			
Assyrian	XY		√			
Azeri (Azerbaijani)	AX		√	√		
Belorussian (aka Byelorussian)	BL		√			
Bengali	BN			√	√	
Bosnian	BX				√	
Bulgarian	BU	√	√		√	
Burmese	BY	√				
Cambodian (Khmer)	CA	√			√	
Cebuano	VB		√	√		
Chavacano	HV			√		

Language	Code					
Chechen	CK		√			
Chinese Cantonese	CC	√	√	√	√	
Chinese Mandarin	CM	√	√	√	√	
Chinese Taiwanese (South Min/Amoy)	CD	√	√			√
Chinese-Wu	CS		√	√		
Croatian	SC				√	
Czech	CX	√	√	√	√	
Danish	DA	√			√	
Dutch	DU	√		√	√	
English	EN		√	√		
Estonian	ES				√	
Finnish	FJ				√	
Flemish	FL				√	
French	FR	√	√	√	√	
Fula/Toucouleur	FV				√	
Georgian	GG				√	
German	GM	√	√	√	√	
Greek	GR	√	√	√	√	
Gujarati	GW				√	
Haitian-Creole	HC			√	√	
Hausa	HS	√				√
Hebrew	HE	√	√	√	√	
Hiligaynon	VH					
Hindi	HJ	√	√	√	√	
Hmong/Mong	MC			√		
Hungarian	HU	√	√		√	
Icelandic	JC	√			√	
Igbo, AKA Ibo				√		
Ilonggo	Not assigned					
Indonesian	JN			√	√	
Italian	JT	√	√		√	
Japanese	JA	√	√	√	√	
Javanese	JV					
Kashmiri	KB					√
Kazakh	KE				√	
Kikongo/Kongo	KG					√
Kirghiz	KM				√	
Korean	KP	√	√	√	√	
Kurdish-Behdini (Kurmanji)	XK		√			
Kurdish-Sorani	XS	√	√		√	
Lao	LC	√			√	
Latvian	LE				√	
Lithuanian	LT	√			√	
Macedonian	MA				√	
Malay	ML			√	√	
Malayalam	MN				√	
Mandingo-Bambara	BA				√	
Marathi	MR				√	
Mongolian	MV				√	
Nepali (Nepalese)	NE				√	
Norwegian	NR	√	√		√	
Pashto-Afghan	PV	√	√	√	√	
Persian-Afghan (Dari)	PG	√	√		√	

Language	Code					
Persian-Farsi	PF	√	√	√	√	
Persian-Tajiki	TB				√	
Polish	PL	√	√		√	
Portugese-Brazilian	PQ	√	√		√	
Portugese-European	PT	√	√		√	
Punjabi (aka Panjabi)	PJ			√	√	
Quechua	QU					
Romanian	RQ	√		√	√	
Russian	RU	√	√	√	√	
Samoan	SA					
Serbian	SC	√			√	
Serbian/Croatian	SC	√	√	√		
Sindhi	SD					√
Singhalese	SJ				√	
Slovak	SK		√	√	√	
Slovenian	SL	√			√	
Somali	SM			√		√
Spanish	QB	√	√	√	√	
Swahili	SW	√		√	√	
Swedish	SY	√			√	
Tagalog	TA	√	√	√	√	
Tamil (Indian)	TC				√	√**
Tausug	MH			√		
Telugu	TE				√	
Thai	TH	√	√		√	
Tibetan	TJ					√
Tigrinya	TL					√
Turkish	TU	√	√	√	√	
Twi				√		
Ukrainian	UK	√	√		√	
Urdu	UR	√	√	√	√	
Uyghur				√		
Uzbek	UX		√		√	
Vietnamese	VN	√	√	√	√	
Visayan	VY					
Wolof	WQ				√	
Yiddish	YJ	√				
Yoruba	YQ			√	√	
Zulu	XU					√

Enclosure (5)

SAMPLE INVENTORY FORMAT

1230
Office Code
Date

From: Classification Test Materiel Custodian, Lifelong Learning
        Center, Marine Corps Base, Quantico, VA
To: Commandant of the Marine Corps (MPP-50)

Subj: CLASSIFICATION TEST MATERIEL SEMI-ANNUAL INVENTORY

Ref: (a) MCO 1230.5B

Encl: (1) Classification Test Materiel Inventory

1. Per the reference, enclosure (1) is submitted for July to
December 2009 semi-annual Classification Test Materiel Inventory.

2. Classification test materiels are stored within three steel
safes with combination locks. Safes are kept in room 237 with
the door locked at all times unless occupied by authorized
personnel designated in writing. Access to room 237 after hours
is prohibited except in the event of an emergency. In the event
of an emergency after hours, emergency personnel must be
accompanied by authorized personnel.

3. Point of Contact in this matter is I. Testalot, comm: (123)
456-7890.

                              I. TESTALOT

SAMPLE INVENTORY FORMAT

TEST	FORM	SKILL	SERIAL #	LOCATION	MEDIA
AFCT	18F	AFCT	00512	CLNC/Safe #1	Booklet
AFCT	19G	AFCT	00342	CLNC/Safe #2	Booklet
Arabic	J	Reading	000123	CLNC/Safe #3	Booklet
Arabic	J	Listening	000123	CLNC/Safe #3	CD
DLAB	B	Reading	00678	CLNC/Safe #1	Booklet
DLAB	b	Listening	00391	CLNC/Safe #1	CD